I pull on my black pirate hat.
I hold tight to my treasure map.

Drop the sail, set out to sea.

Rain and mist sweep right past me.

The Pirate Quest

Written by Amy Sparkes
Illustrated by Dan Widdowson

I am on a quest, to find a wooden chest!

A squid swims by, a shoal of fish ...

I hear the waves go swish, swish, swish.

Then with a crash, my boat hits land.

I feel afraid. I step on the sand.

Thick weeds loom up from the deep.

Shells crick-crack under my feet.

But right at the back, I spot a chest …

I am the champion of the pirate quest!

Talk about the story

Ask your child these questions:

1 What was the girl in the story looking for?

2 Who sailed in the boat with the girl?

3 Why did the shells make a crick-crack noise?

4 Was the girl actually a pirate? How do you know?

5 What treasure would you like to find inside a treasure chest?

6 Have you ever used a map to help you find your way somewhere?

Can your child retell the story in their own words?